THE THOUGHT OF THE OLD TESTAMENT

THE THOUGHT
OF THE
OLD TESTAMENT

Three Lectures

BY

C. R. NORTH

WIPF & STOCK · Eugene, Oregon

Wipf and Stock Publishers
199 W 8th Ave, Suite 3
Eugene, OR 97401

The Thought of the Old Testament
By North, Christopher R.
Copyright©1948 Epworth Press
ISBN 13: 978-1-60608-712-1
Publication date 1/8/2014
Previously published by Epworth Press, 1948

Copyright © Epworth Press 1948
First English edition1948 by Epworth Press
This edition published by arrangement with Epworth Press

CONTENTS

FOREWORD 7

1. GOD 9
   Preliminaries: Old Testament thought: (a) Not philosophical. (b) Not systematized. (c) Not chronologically arranged.
   'I AM THAT I AM': God not in process of becoming—History the Medium of Revelation.
   The Covenant Relationship: Not a legal transaction—Desscribed in terms of (a) Bridegroom-bride. (b) Father-son. (c) King-subject.
   Emphasis on God as Redeemer rather than as Creator. Old Testament religion a religion of Grace.

2. THE WORLD 26
   Man: His uniqueness in creation—'An animated body, not an incarnated soul'—Conception of human nature not dualistic—Old Testament psychology.
   Nature: Natural phenomena 'acts of God'. No divine immanence.
   God's Relation to the World: Complicated by sin—Issue as between Judaism and Christianity—Theophanies—'The angel of Yahweh'—The prophetic 'Word'—'The spirit of Yahweh'—Wisdom.

3. SALVATION 44
   Moral evil and its remedies: Sin primarily rebellion—The moral law—The Sacrificial System—Forgiveness—Law and sacrifice not to establish covenant-relation but to maintain it —General similarity between Old Testament and New Testament.
   Corporate emphasis in Old Testament religion: The Kingdom of God—'The Day of Yahweh'—Attitude to Gentiles—Principle of Retributive Righteousness—The Future Life—The Messiah—The Suffering Servant.

FOREWORD

THE lectures here printed were given in Swansea last year, at an Easter Vacation School organized by the Welsh Department of the Ministry of Education. There is nothing very new in them, though some questions raised in Lecture II may be worth anyone's consideration. They outline the faith of the Old Testament in the centuries immediately preceding the rise of Christianity. They are not a sketch of the history of Hebrew religion, though they do emphasize the fact that Old Testament religion arose out of certain crises of history, not as a deliberate attempt to formulate doctrine. The doctrine is the necessary outcome of a nation's religious experience. The main themes dealt with are God, the world and God's relation to it, and the problem of evil and its remedy. The conclusion reached is that Old Testament religion was, in its essential principles, as much a religion of grace as that of the New, that there is a general parallelism between the leading ideas of the two Testaments, most of what is commonly regarded as peculiar to Christianity being already foreshadowed in the religion of Israel.

The lectures are printed exactly as they were delivered. It is my hope that they may be useful to teachers and students in the present dearth of textbooks, especially on Old Testament theology.

C. R. NORTH.

BANGOR,
Epiphany, 1948.

GOD

THE subject on which I have been asked to lecture to you is 'The Thought of the Old Testament', to which there is added, by way of a further directive, 'especially as leading up to the New'. I take it that what you want from me is some account of the Old Testament interpretation of life and the universe; that your main interest is in the New Testament, for which, you assume, the Old is essentially a preparation; and that you wish me to put you in the position in which you may, from the vantage point of the Old Testament, the better understand the New. You frankly recognize that the thought of the New Testament is only partially intelligible to the man who knows nothing about the Old. As it is often said, 'The New Testament is implicit in the Old; the Old Testament is explicit in the New.' That, of course, is perfectly true. The Old Testament, taken by itself, is incomplete; it constantly looks forward beyond itself. At the same time, by way of comment on a possible wrong emphasis in your 'especially as leading up to the New Testament', I should like to state my conviction that the Old Testament is worthy of serious study for its own sake, quite apart from its value as a preparation for the New, and that we are not doing it justice if we only use it as a ladder to be kicked down when we think it has served its purpose. I could wish that the average citizen today had as sane and balanced a view of life and destiny as is presented in the Old Testament.

Before we proceed farther, I wish to make three preliminary observations on the main theme, 'The Thought of the Old Testament'.

(1) The Old Testament contains little that would pass for 'thought' in the department of philosophy of a modern university. Such philosophy as we find in it is moral rather than intellectual. By that I do not mean that the ancient Hebrews were not an intellectually gifted people. They were; though the only art in which they excelled was the art of writing. The Old Testament is superb literature. But nowhere does it attempt to build up a system of thought on the basis of pure reason. That sort of endeavour we owe to the Greeks. You can put the broad difference between the Greek and Hebrew ways of approaching reality if you say that the Greek began with Nature, while the Hebrew began with God. For him God was not the conclusion of a syllogism, nor, indeed, of any inductive argument. He did not, like Descartes, first reduce all presuppositions to the dimensions of 'I think, therefore I am', and then proceed to reach God by a lengthy chain of reasoning. God, for him, was not, as He is for many philosophers, the great 'Perhaps'. He was the presupposition on which all else depended. We might perhaps put it that the Hebrew apprehension of God was intuitive rather than ratiocinative, though even that way of expressing it is not altogether free from objections. In the last resort, man didn't reach out to God at all; rather was it God who reached out to and apprehended man, confronting man in the concrete situations of his life.

(2) My second preliminary observation is that even such 'thought' as we find in the Old Testament is nowhere set out in systematized form. Not only were the Hebrews not philosophers; they were not even systematic theologians. Their concern was with religion rather than with theology. There is plenty of theology in the Old Testament. But the business of reducing it to something like a system is a task which, if we think it worth while attempting, we must undertake for ourselves.

(3) My third preliminary observation is closely related to my second. It is this: it is no longer possible to assume that the order of the books in the Old Testament is, even approximately, the order in which they were composed. Moses did not write the Pentateuch, neither did Joshua and Samuel write the books that are called by their names; David did not write most of the Psalms, nor did Solomon compose most of Proverbs. Malachi, the last book in the Old Testament, which probably dates from the first half of the fifth century B.C., was not the last book to be written. Some parts of the prophetical writings, and a good deal of the Pentateuch, are later than Malachi. Indeed, the general theological standpoint of the Old Testament is that of the post-exilic age, rather later than the time of Malachi. Most of the longer books are composite—that is to say, they contain materials from different sources, which sometimes differ in age by as much as centuries. Some parts of the Old Testament may well have been written as early as the 9th or 10th century B.C., and they rest upon oral tradition which is earlier still. But we cannot assume that because a passage is in the Pentateuch, therefore it is early; it may well be

even later than Malachi. It is obviously impossible for me, in the course of three lectures, to indicate, even summarily, which parts of the literature are early, and which are late. That is the task of documentary, or, as it is often called, the 'Higher' criticism, and it is not the task you have assigned to me. But I should like to say, in parenthesis, that the recognition that most of the books in the Old Testament are of composite authorship has greatly exercised the minds of scholars for now nearly two hundred years. Enormous labour has been expended in trying to arrange the materials in chronological order. It is clear that many of the early religious conceptions of the Hebrews were primitive and crude, and partly in order that these primitive conceptions might be seen in their true perspective in relation to later and more spiritual developments, scholars have preferred to write histories of Hebrew religion rather than theologies of the Old Testament. In the circumstances, that was entirely necessary. But now there is a growing disposition to say that we have had enough histories of Old Testament religion, and that what we want is Old Testament theology. That is what you, whether you realize it or not, are asking from me when you invite me to lecture on the Thought of the Old Testament. I shall try to do that by giving you, as it were, a cross-section of Jewish conceptions about God and the world in the post-exilic age, when, as I have said, the Old Testament assumed its present form. And if I do that I shall be obeying your directive to treat the subject 'especially as leading up to the New Testament'. Because the later centuries B.C. are sufficiently near to the Christian era to stand upon its threshold. And if the picture I give you turns out to be, perhaps, rather less objectionable and more attractive than you had expected—if, for example, I say little about such stories as that which is told of God's commanding Saul to exterminate the Amalekites—pray do not accuse me afterwards of having given you a one-sided picture, of keeping dark features which may seem to give the lie to what I do say. You have asked me for a summary of Old Testament thought, not for an historical sketch of Hebrew religion. My standpoint is broadly that of the fifth and fourth centuries B.C., on the threshold of the Christian era, when most of the early crudities had been outgrown. That is to say, we are to look forward in the direction of Christianity, rather than backward in the direction of primitive animism. If I were to attempt to be so inclusive as to tell you that God was a vengeful Deity who demanded the indiscriminate slaughter of innocent women and children, and at the same time so gracious and full of compassion that He had pity on the very babes and cattle of Nineveh, then I should be giving you a distorted, cross-eyed picture.

So much by way of preliminaries.

Now, if Hebrew thought began and ended with God, if, that is to say, it was theocentric, it is obvious that we must begin with the Old Testament conception of God.

In some ways the most revealing passage about God in the Old Testament is the one in Exodus 3 which tells how, when God commissioned Moses to go and deliver the Israelites from Egypt, Moses asked, 'Behold, when I come unto the children of Israel, and shall say unto them, The God of your fathers hath sent me unto you; and they shall say unto me, What is his name? What shall I say unto them?' God's answer was—according to both the standard English versions: 'I AM THAT I AM.... Thus shalt thou say unto the children of Israel, I AM hath sent me unto you.' The passage is generally dated to approximately the eighth century B.C. And here I should say that although the general standpoint of these lectures is three or four centuries later than that, this eighth-century text may still be quoted as evidence of what the Hebrews thought of God in the fifth century, and, for that matter, what they still think of Him today. Some ideas of God that were current in the early centuries had their roots in primitive animism; they were gradually sloughed off. Others were found in experience to accord with eternal truth; instead of being superseded they were retained, and even came to have a fuller content with the passage of the centuries. This is one of them: 'I AM THAT I AM . . . I AM hath sent me unto you.' For the words 'I AM THAT I AM' the margin of the Revised Version has three alternatives, of which the third, 'I WILL BE THAT I WILL BE', is by general consent the best. What the name Yahweh (as we pronounce it) originally meant we do not know. But by the eighth century it had come to have the meaning, 'He will be'. It was what modern grammarians parse as the third person singular of the imperfect—and translate by the future —of the verb 'to be'. So if God spoke of Himself, He called Himself 'I will be' (*Ehyeh*). If men spoke of Him they called Him 'He will be' (*Yahweh*).

Now the Hebrew word rendered 'to be' had not quite the same meaning as our 'to be'. It had rather the meaning 'to become', 'to fall out', 'to happen'.

If you know any Greek, it corresponded to *ginesthai* rather than to *'einai*. Though, again, we must be careful: if we render 'Yahweh' as 'He who will become', we must not imagine that the Hebrews thought of God as in process of becoming, after the fashion of some modern philosophies of emergent evolution. True, there is progressive development in the Hebrew idea of God; there was nothing static about Hebrew religion, at least during its creative period—say, from Moses to Deutero-Isaiah. Deutero-Isaiah, as we call him, the great Prophet of the Exile, had a more profound conception of God than previous ages, even than Moses, had had. But no Hebrew would for a moment have entertained the idea, so widespread in these days, that God is in process of becoming, or growing with the growth of the human race, as we often flatter ourselves He is doing. God was not man; God was God, and man was man. God was before man. God created man. Nevertheless, if we translate Yahweh as 'He who is'—or, better, with the Revised Version margin, 'He who will be'—the emphasis is not so much upon the One who exists essentially, the Self-existent, Greek *ho 'ôn*. 'I will be what I will be', 'I will become what I will become'. No! the sentence is really untranslatable, so we had better, after all, stick to 'He will be'. But the emphasis lies not upon God's abstract Being, but upon the fact that He meets Israel in the course of its history, and will continue to do so. I am fain to admit that by the fifth century B.C., which is our general *pou stô*, or century of observation, Judaism was beginning to look mainly to the past, to the age of Moses; in other words, it was beginning to systematize. But the predominant attitude or stance during the age of the great prophets was in the direction of the future rather than toward the past. To refer again to the call of Moses: Moses, you remember, made every excuse he could think of to evade the divine commission: 'Who am I, that I should go unto Pharaoh, and that I should bring forth the children of Israel out of Egypt?' And Yahweh said, 'Certainly I will be'—note the play on the divine name—'I will be with thee; and this shall be the token that it is I who have sent thee: When thou hast brought forth the people out of Egypt, ye shall serve God upon this mountain.' In other words, 'When you have done what I tell you, then you shall know that it is I who have sent you.' It may seem odd to us, like putting the cart before the horse. Though really it is true: as Jesus said, 'If any man willeth to do God's will, he shall know of the teaching'. That is characteristic of the Old Testament attitude to and conception of God. God is not a proposition to be discussed. He does not hold forth about His attributes, or describe what He is like. He lays hold on men in the crises of their lives. He brings about crises in their lives. History is His primary medium of revelation, not speeches. God is known for what He is by what He does.

What does He do? He calls Abraham to leave Ur of the Chaldees and to journey to a land that he knows not (there you have an excellent illustration of the principle, 'I will be what I will be'); He comes to deliver the Israelites from slavery in Egypt (the Exodus in the Old Testament corresponds to the Resurrection in the New); when His people persistently break faith with Him, He calls in the Assyrians or the Babylonians to chastise them, to destroy their kingdom, and to carry them off into exile; He raises up the Persian conqueror Cyrus to deliver them from exile. . . . These were the crises in history which became indelibly inscribed upon the racial memory of the Hebrews, and it was through them that the character of God was known.

You will notice that although non-Israelite peoples, Assyrians, Babylonians, and Persians, enter into the picture, they are on the circumference of it rather than at its centre. Their role is incidental to Yahweh's primary purpose, which was with Israel. The fact is that the Hebrews did not set out to formulate a doctrine of God from universal premises—they were, indeed, in no position to survey mankind from China to Peru; they were not, even, when they first came into contact with Yahweh, strict monotheists—they began with their experience of God's dealings with them as a people, and they never, in Old Testament times, quite outgrew their nationalist conception of religion. (Indeed, perhaps, the Jews have never quite outgrown it since.) Even when by the fifth century B.C., they had become strict monotheists, and therefore perforce had to assign to Gentiles some place in their total view of life, their explanation was that the Creator had deliberately selected out of all the races of mankind one people—namely, themselves—the descendants of Jacob the grandson of Abraham, to be peculiarly His own, and to live in what they called a covenant-relation to Him. We may be tempted, when we hear that, to exclaim that the whole idea of a chosen nation is preposterous, that, of course, the Hebrews were generalizing from inadequate premises, and that their view of God and His relation to the world has therefore no more than an antiquarian and historical interest. But before we hastily do that let us at least inquire what the covenant-relation implied. It may very well turn out that the truths it contains are valid in a wider setting, as indeed the New Testament asserts that they are.

Very well, then: the Hebrews did not begin with abstract thought; they began with life, with life as they as a people, a corporate entity, experienced it. Yahweh delivered them from Egyptian slavery, and entered into convenant with them to be their God and they His people. Some Old Testament passages, and quite early ones at that, date back Yahweh's covenant with Israel even to the time of Abraham. It is important that we should understand that the covenant was not a crude bargain. The misconception is widely current—partly due to what St. Paul in the heat of controversy had to say about the Law—that Yahweh's covenant relation to Israel was a purely legal transaction. That is a gross exaggeration. In point of fact, it was in origin the most intimate and tender of all relationships. The prophets Hosea and Jeremiah, especially, describe it in terms of the marriage bond. Courtship among the Hebrews may have been less romantic than it is with us, but we have no reason to suppose that marriage, in the long run, was conspicuously less happy with them than it is with us. Certainly Hosea loved his wife, even though she was unfaithful to him. Jeremiah never married; not because he was morose, a misogynist: on the contrary, the phrase 'the voice of the bridegroom and the voice of the bride' was so often on his lips that we may be quite sure that he often longed for a companionship which, he felt, God had denied him. Hosea and Jeremiah pictured

Yahweh's relationship to Israel under the figure of the marriage bond. The emotional tie that bound Yahweh and Israel to one another in loyalty was one which was expressed by the almost untranslatable word *ḥesed*, usually rendered in the English Bible, not very adequately, 'lovingkindness'. The word 'devotion' expresses as well as any this reciprocal attitude, Yahweh's *ḥesed* toward Israel and Israel's *ḥesed* toward Yahweh. Frequently joined with devotion is 'faithfulness' or 'fidelity'.

The negative counterpart of *ḥesed*, this conjugal devotion and fidelity, is 'jealousy'. We bridle up when we read, 'Yahweh thy God is a jealous God'. But the one figure is entirely consistent with the other. Granted that Yahweh's relationship to Israel is that of Bridegroom to bride, Yahweh is naturally 'jealous' and 'angry' if Israel, His wife, to continue the figure, commits adultery by forsaking Him for other gods. (At this point it may be pertinent to remark that since the Hebrews derived their conceptions of God, not from abstract categories, but from their concrete experience of life, they were bound to use anthropomorphic language when they attempted to describe Him.) To be sure, the Bridegroom-bride figure was a risky one to use, and we may wonder why the prophets ever used it, since it was so patently open to misconception and abuse. It was a common figure in the Nature-worship with which the Hebrews came into contact when they entered Canaan. The agricultural deities of Canaan were called Baals, and Baal means 'lord', 'owner', 'husband' (as 'lord' or 'owner' of his wife). The idea was that the Baal was the husband of the soil, the god being the male and the soil the female principle. It can easily be seen that this conception gave plenty of scope for sexual licence and even ritual prostitution, the idea, on the principle that like produces like, being that these practices assisted the god in his task of imparting fertility to the soil. The prophets loathed the whole sordid business. Nevertheless, they kept the figure of Bridegroom and bride when they wanted to describe the relation between Yahweh and Israel; but with this difference: that for Baal-worship the female principle was the *soil*, for Yahwism it was the *people* Israel. Moreover, while for Baalism the relationship between the god and the land was one that existed in *nature* and from time immemorial, for Yahwism it was the outcome of *grace*, the grace and compassion that had delivered Israel from Egypt, an event in history. Do you see how inaccurate it is to speak as though the bond that united Israel and Yahweh was only a legal bond? Instead, Old Testament religion is in its way, and with the qualification that it was a national rather than a universal faith, as much a religion of grace as New Testament religion is. All the same, as I have said, the marriage figure was a risky one for the prophets to use, and by the fifth century B.C. it had ceased to have much prominence in Jewish piety. Still, when the Psalmists wished to describe God's love and grace, as they constantly do, they praised His *ḥesed*, His lovingkindness, His loyalty, His devotion, and His faithfulness, in language that goes back to the ancient figure of Yahweh the Husband and Israel the bride. And when the New Testament wishes to extol Christ's love for the Church, it calls the Church the bride, the wife of the Lamb.

Another figure which the prophets, particularly

Hosea, use to describe Yahweh's relationship to Israel is that of Father and son. Yahweh was Father; Israel was His son. 'When Israel was a child, then I came to love him and called my son out of Egypt (Hosea 11[1]). The prophet goes on to report Yahweh as saying that He had taught Israel to walk. Again, this conception of the Father-son relationship between Yahweh and Israel has its parallel in primitive paganism. Many peoples believed that they were the actual physical descendants of their gods. The prophets retained the figure, but once more with a significant difference: Israel's sonship to Yahweh was not something that existed in Nature, it had its beginning in a definite historical event—namely, the Exodus; 'When Israel was a child, then I came to love him, and called my son out of Egypt'. In other words, Israel's sonship was not a natural or inevitable sonship; it was rather a sonship of adoption. It began to be, just as the Bridegroom-bride relationship began to be. It could therefore conceivably be terminated if Israel on its part was unfaithful to its filial obligations. The emotional tie which bound Yahweh and Israel in the Father-son relationship was love and pity on God's part, and a responsive love, not unmingled with reverence and fear, on the part of Israel. 'Like as a father pitieth his children, so the Lord pitieth them that fear him' (Psalm 103[13]). Love to Yahweh is enjoined upon Israel as a command: 'Thou shalt love the Lord thy God.' Again, very much as with the marriage figure, there was a tendency, in the days after the exile, when God came to be conceived more and more as transcendent and remote from the world, for the Father-son figure to recede into the background. Not altogether, of course, if only because the language of ancient piety was retained: 'Thou, O Lord, art our Father; our Redeemer from everlasting is thy name' (Isaiah 63[16]). But the doctrine of the divine Fatherhood was limited in Old Testament times in that Yahweh was the Father of Israel, not of all mankind; also, He was the Father of the nation Israel rather than of the individual Israelite. In the New Testament the barrier to individual sonship is broken down: 'As many as received him, to them gave he [Jesus] the right to become children of God, even to them that believe on his name.' But even in the New Testament, as the text shows clearly, God is hardly depicted as the Father of all men, irrespective of their response in filial love to Him. Men are not, without further ado, the children of God by nature. Christian sonship is a sonship of adoption, as the sonship of Israel was in the Old Testament. 'Ye received the spirit of adoption, whereby we cry, Abba, Father' (Romans 8[15]). We are the children of God by His infinite grace and mercy. And just as in the Old Testament Israel was commanded to love God, it is nowise different with the individual Christian in the New. Jesus took over from the Old Testament the word, 'Thou shalt love the Lord thy God with all thy heart, and with all thy soul, and with all thy mind, and with all thy strength', and added that it was the great and first commandment.

We have seen that there was, in later Old Testament times, a tendency for the more human and anthropomorphic conceptions of God's relationship to men to recede into the background. As they did so, the conception of Yahweh as King, which was equally ancient with them, came more and more into prominence. Even so, the King-subject figure did not lie altogether outside the general covenant idea, since in the Hebrew institution of monarchy the relationship between the king and his subjects was based upon a covenant, with mutual rights and obligations on both sides. Nevertheless, to think of Yahweh as King, and Israel as His loyal and obedient subjects, was less open to abuse as encouraging over-familiarity on man's part with God than the ideas centring round the conceptions of marriage and paternity were. Hence it is broadly true to say that the Jew in post-exilic times, when the Old Testament reached its present final form, pictured Yahweh more readily as King than he did as Husband or Father. The character of Yahweh as King was bound up with the thought of His Righteousness and Holiness—holiness being not simply moral purity, though it included that, but majestic exaltation and even unapproachableness, to which man's response was one of reverence and awe, mingled with a sense of his own finitude and creatureliness and moral impurity. The classic text is to be found in the account of Isaiah's vision in the Temple: when he saw Yahweh in majestic exaltation and heard the 'Holy, holy, holy' of the seraphim, Isaiah was smitten with shame and self-abasement, and cried out, 'Woe is me, for I am condemned, because I am a man of unclean lips, and I dwell in the midst of a people of unclean lips, for the King, Yahweh of hosts, have my eyes seen' (Isaiah 6[5]). The epithet 'Yahweh of hosts' was a natural accompaniment of the thought of Yahweh as King. It was an ancient title, but whereas in the early days the 'hosts' had been the armies of Israel, they later came to be thought of as the stars, His martial retinue. Yahweh was Lord. Gradually men came to feel that there was something presumptuous and irreverent in calling Him by His personal name at all. Yahweh became 'Lord' simply, until the original pronunciation of the name was forgotten, or words like 'Heaven', or 'the Name', or 'the Blessed' were substituted for it; that is why in St. Matthew, the most Jewish of the Gospels, we read of 'the Kingdom of heaven' rather than the Kingdom of God.

I read a book recently in which the writer described the Hebrew conception of God as 'transcendental monotheism . . . the product of the abstract intellect'. He says that 'lofty as this conception was, it was abstract and seemed to remove God from human relations'. That is surely a gross exaggeration. There may be an element of truth in it. By the end of the Old Testament period God was becoming, perhaps, rather remote, but even so I should deny that the conception of Him was 'abstract'. Certainly it was not abstract in origin, a product of the abstract intellect. The Old Testament doctrine of God was the Hebrews' response to God's confronting of them in the crises, the deliverances, and disasters of their national life during a thousand years of history. Of course, however you come by your experience of God, you are bound, if you think long and hard enough, to attempt to formulate some philosophy of His being. 'I will be what I will be' (or 'become', or however one should attempt to translate it) must inevitably become 'Jehovah! Great I AM', and man's mind would only be shirking its duty if it did not go on to frame some such conception of ultimate reality. Not that the Jews in Old Testament times did that in philosophical terms, though many Jewish philosophers have attempted it since. Instead, in the centuries immediately preceding the Christian era, God did on the whole become more remote, both in space and time. Attempts were made to fill up the vacuum created by His increasing transcendence in relation to the world by conceptions of mediators of one kind and another between Him and the world. Who or what these mediators were there is not time to describe in this lecture; and besides, the subject is perhaps better left over until we have tried to see how the Jews thought of the world to which God needed or chose to reveal Himself. By the beginning of the Christian era Judaism had accomplished its main task, and if there was a danger that God might become permanently an absentee from the world He had created, Christianity, with its doctrine of the Incarnation, provided the perfect Mediator, and brought God back into direct relation to history, in which the Hebrews had first met Him, and thus saved monotheism from the peril of degenerating into stark deism.

You may perhaps have noticed that in this lecture I have said nothing about God as Creator. That is partly because the doctrine of creation is best treated in relation to Hebrew thought of the world which God created, but more because in the Hebrew experience of God the conception of God as Creator is secondary in importance to the conception of Him as Saviour and Redeemer. Of course, in the Old Testament Yahweh is Creator; the first chapter of the Bible is an account of the creation. But it was as Saviour that the Hebrews first came to know Yahweh. For us the logical and chronological order of thought is Creator-Saviour. For the living faith of the Old Testament it was the reverse. The Hebrews did not begin by formulating a doctrine of creation, and then go on to ask whether the Creator was also Saviour. It was the Saviour-God who had taken hold of them at the Exodus, and for them the order was Saviour-Creator. The Old Testament and New Testament are at one in placing Salvation and Redemption at the centre of their message. Creation is by comparison almost an afterthought. I said at the outset that the Hebrews were neither philosophers nor systematic theologians. I like to think that they put first things first. I believe they did.

II

THE WORLD

THERE are two accounts of creation in the Old Testament. In the first (Genesis 1) man is last in the order of created things; in the second (Genesis 2) he is first. Both accounts agree in making him the crown and summit of creation: he is to 'subdue' the earth, and to have dominion over all the creatures (Genesis 1[28]; cf. Psalm 8[6-8]). This emphasis upon man's uniqueness in the scale of creation is evident from the fact that in the first creation story God announces to His heavenly council His intention to make man 'in our image, after our likeness' (Genesis 1[26]—the 'our' is not to be taken as an adumbration of the Christian doctrine of the Trinity); similarly, in Psalm 8 it is said that God made man 'but little lower than God' (Revised Version).

'In our image, after our likeness' probably refers to man's bodily form, 'godlike, erect'. God was supposed to have a 'form' (Exodus 33$^{20-3}$); the prohibition to make any 'image' of Him is not a denial of this, but rather a confirmation. The difference between God and man is not one of form, but of substance: man is flesh, God is spirit (Isaiah 31^3).

The second and more naïve story of creation describes how God 'formed man of the dust of the ground, and breathed into his nostrils the breath of life, and man became a living soul' (*nephesh*, Genesis 2^7). This very anthropomorphic account was not exactly rendered obsolete when the later account, which eschews all anthropomorphisms, was written. Even in the Book of Job (Job 10$^{10f.}$) and in certain late psalms (especially 139$^{13-16}$) the individual birth is described as the result of direct divine activity, though it is open to us to suppose that the details are intended figuratively. The Genesis passage, which is quite in agreement with the Old Testament generally, has been defined as implying that 'man is an animated body, not an incarnated soul'. In this it is in direct contrast with the Greek view, which, speaking broadly, we have inherited— namely, that man is an immortal soul temporarily housed or imprisoned in an earthly body. But I put it to you that the Hebrew view, naïve though it may seem, may have something to say for itself in the light of modern psychology. I have not observed that my children, when they are born, are so many pieces of ready-made 'soul-stuff' brought out from somewhere in the unseen and lodged in bodies which are not part of their true 'selves'. Instead, for a good many years at any rate, the soul, or whatever we should properly call it, grows with the growth of the body. Anyhow, whichever of the two conceptions of human personality, the Greek or the Hebrew, is the right one, according to the Hebrew view of his constitution, man was an animated body, and the body was an equal partner in the alliance of body and soul. So much so was the body an integral part of human nature that, paradoxically, the Hebrews had no regular word for it; this because the body was so perfectly obvious to them that they did not feel that they needed a special word to mark the contrast between it and the *nephesh* or soul.

From this it follows that the Old Testament conception of human nature was not dualistic, as ours inclines to be. The Hebrews had no doubt about the reality of evil, but they did not locate it specifically in 'the flesh'. Hence, their religion was not rigorously ascetic. They saw no virtue in celibacy, for example. They had their fasts, especially during and after the exile, when calamity was their major portion. But they did not indulge in fastings and penances overmuch, or for the purpose of degrading their bodies. This was a good world; God had pronounced it so when He created it, and He meant men to enjoy it, though not, of course, to make beasts of themselves.

I have spoken about the debatable issue as between the Greek and Hebrew conceptions of human personality, and indicated my view that the Hebrew conception is not to be dismissed out of hand. But much Hebrew psychology is antiquated, though no more so than any other psychology that is not strictly modern. This does not mean that we can afford to neglect it altogether; indeed, it is an extremely fascinating subject. Human nature has changed but little since Old Testament times, and if we will take the trouble to learn the essential features of Hebrew psychology, and then translate them into terms of our modern psychology, we shall be well rewarded; because the Hebrews did understand human character and motives, no matter how elementary their psychology may have been. Briefly, the Hebrews knew nothing about either the respiratory system or the circulation of the blood, nor did they know anything about the functions of the brain; even the Syrians, a kindred people whose literature dates from the Christian era, and who were more sophisticated than the Hebrews, knew nothing more about the brain than to call it 'the marrow of the head'. And now, if the Hebrews did not think with their heads, or did not know that they did, what did they think they thought with? What did they feel with? For them the heart was the seat of the intellect and the will, and the bowels and the kidneys ('reins' in the English Bible) were, mainly, the seat of the emotions. This, of course, is 'functional' psychology and it is quite obsolete. We still speak in terms of it, especially when we use devotional language, though we do not always translate the Old Testament terms aright. For example, we preachers beseech men to give their hearts to God, and they think we mean—perhaps we sometimes do mean—that they are to give to God their emotions. But when the prophet Hosea accused the Israelites of being 'heartless' (Hosea 7^{11}), he meant that they were witless, stupid; and when Jesus, who, as a Jew, naturally thought in Old Testament terms, said, 'Blessed are the pure in heart, for they shall see God', He was thinking not so much of those who are sexually chaste—which is what the words most readily convey to us—but of those whose minds and wills are sincere.

The Hebrew conception of Nature and the universe was, it goes without saying, pre-Copernican. The earth was the centre of the universe. Over it was a dome-shaped 'firmament' or cupola, the purpose of which was 'to divide the waters from the waters' (Genesis 1[6]), to prevent the waters of abysmal chaos from breaking in upon the ordered world. There is no explicit assertion in the Old Testament that creation was 'out of nothing'. What God did was to bring cosmos out of the primeval chaos. Of this primeval chaos the turbulent sea was a kind of symbol, and when in the description of the new Jerusalem in the New Testament Book of Revelation (Revelation 21[1]) it is said that 'the sea is no more', the meaning is that the peril that the inhabited earth might return to the original chaos is forever removed. There is no need for me to attempt a detailed account of Hebrew cosmology. Much of it is very picturesque; for example, in Psalm 104, which is a poetic parallel to the prose account of creation in Genesis 1, with its description (verse 3) of Yahweh's heavenly dwelling resting upon piles driven deep down into the abyss; but the details are not strictly relevant to the thought of the Old Testament. So long as we do not run away with the idea that because Hebrew conceptions of the nature of the physical universe are pre-scientific, therefore the Old Testament is an entirely obsolete book, we may let them stand, and even take delight in their fancies. And after all, no matter how many extra-galactic nebulae wait to be discovered by our telescopes, no more magnificent descriptions of the creative power of God are ever likely to be written than those we have in Isaiah 40 and Job 38. No scientific discoveries will ever outdate the broad sweep of these passages; they comprehend and even swallow up all that atomic or any other science is ever likely to say.

It must freely be granted that the Hebrew universe was a very miniature affair compared with the universe as we know it. Every natural phenomenon was a direct 'act of God'. The Hebrews knew little or nothing of secondary causes, 'laws of Nature' as we call them. Thunder was the voice of Yahweh, and the lightnings were His arrows. Amos had no hesitation in making Yahweh say, 'I caused it to rain upon one city, and caused it not to rain upon another city: one piece was rained upon, and the piece whereon it rained not withered . . . yet have ye not returned unto me, saith Yahweh'; almost as though God withheld rain for the deliberate purpose of recalling men's attention to their sins, and bringing them to repentance. He would be a bold and—we may think—rather old-fashioned preacher who took that text to point a moral in our recent distresses. For us Nature, as we call it, is strictly impersonal and entirely non-moral. If it hits us hard, it never occurs to us to search our consciences. For the Hebrews it was the instrument of a moral purpose. I wonder if perchance they were right. Thoughtful people are beginning to recognize that our contemporary distresses are the evidences, at bottom, of a moral problem. 'Yet have ye not returned unto me, saith the Lord.' Can anyone deny that the prospect before us would be brighter if we did? We cannot, of course, do that to order, nor in despite of intellectual honesty. But are we altogether right when we look upon Nature simply as a brute, inert thing, to be either defiantly assailed or stoically subdued? Should not the Old Testament remind us that what we call Nature, in the broad sweep of its processes, is the instrument of a personal and purposive Will; that the nexus between God—if God is a moral Being—and ourselves, who are moral beings, is not likely to be completely amoral in its functions? It is worth pondering.

The Hebrews knew nothing of the modern concept of divine immanence. Still less were they pantheists. Their major emphasis was upon the divine transcendence. God was not the 'soul of the universe', as poets since Wordsworth have described Him. He did, as we have already seen, act directly upon Nature, at any time and at any point. He was omnipresent, but He was not immanent. It has been said that no Hebrew poet could ever have written that 'Nature never did betray the heart that loved her'. In that sense, Nature for the Hebrews was more impersonal than she is for us. Nature as such, despite the fact that it might be charged with warnings for men, had no life of its own; it stood over against God, separate from Him. Hebrew Nature poetry is therefore descriptive, not interpretative, as the best Nature poetry is with us. It may scintillate, but it lacks the atmospheric, mystic quality that we have come to expect of it in our rainy climate, where the shadows are cast by distant clouds rather than in hard lines by objects close at hand. But what Hebrew poetry lacks in subtlety it more than makes up in majesty, since all of it that has been preserved— with the exception of the Song of Songs—is intended to extol the glory of God and to sing the praise of His handiwork.

One very difficult, perhaps the most difficult, problem for the philosophy of religion is concerned with God's relation to the world. Face to face with God, man is in the presence of a mystery both tremendous and fascinating. We are drawn on to seek God, and yet God seems utterly unapproachable; unapproachable for two reasons: that He is infinite and we are finite, and that He is holy and we are sinful, or however we should describe our sense of being in the wrong before God. This problem is sometimes starkly obvious in the pages of the Old Testament.

As we saw in the first lecture, there was a certain intimacy and family feeling about the early Hebrew experience of Yahweh, even though Yahweh was always, in the last resort, transcendent to, and different from, Israel. With the passage of time, more and more emphasis came to be laid upon the divine transcendence, notwithstanding that the Jews continued to think of themselves as peculiarly the people of Yahweh, and of Yahweh as residing in their midst, specifically in the Temple, which was His earthly dwelling. 'I will be what I will be' was bound ultimately to be conceived as 'the Great I AM'. The tension between the nearness and the remoteness of man's relation to God becomes on the whole more acute as we approach the Christian era. As I say, there are two factors which complicate the problem, which is religious as well as philosophical, religious before it is philosophical, and, in the Old Testament, religious rather than philosophical; namely God's infinitude over against man's finitude, and His holiness over against man's sinfulness.

Speaking generally, the post-exilic age in Judaism was marked by a deepened sense of sin as compared with the centuries before the exile. I do not propose to deal this evening specifically with the Old Testament teaching about sin, individual and corporate, and its forgiveness; we shall be considering that tomorrow. I only mention sin at the moment as a factor which complicates the relation between God and the world. The Old Testament has a deep sense of the reality, of the sinfulness, of sin. But I think it is true to say that the story of the Fall in Genesis 3 had not the emphasis in the Old Testament that we commonly assume that it had, or that it has had, speaking generally, in Christian theology. Moreover, although in the period immediately preceding the Christian era the story of the Fall did come to have increasing prominence, it has never figured so largely in Jewish as it has in Christian thought. I want, if I can, to put you in the position of being able to understand the problem of the relation of God to the world as it appeared to the pious Jew in the centuries immediately preceding the Christian era, and I think I can best do it with reference to the problem as it exists, and may be argued, as between Judaism and Christianity today.

There is God, and here is man. God is infinite, man is finite; God is holy, man is sinful, or imperfect, if that is the adjective you prefer to use. Now, according to Christianity, God has provided the perfect Mediator between Himself and man, in the God-man, Jesus Christ. For Christianity, the religious problem is therefore solved, and we may leave the philosophical problem, if it remains over, to the philosophers. But the Jews did not, and do not, accept Christ; and, having rejected Him, they have had to adjust their conceptions of the relation between God and the world accordingly.

Whether, in order to do this, they have broken seriously with their own past, as that past is mirrored in the Old Testament, is a matter for argument. They, of course, insist that they haven't. They say that the gulf between God and man is not so wide as Christianity, with its doctrines of original sin and the mediatorial work of Christ, asserts. Not that they any longer say harsh things about Jesus. For them the villain of the piece is the renegade Jew Paul, with his emphasis upon the sin of Adam and its consequences for the race. And, as I have said, to do them justice, the story of the Fall is not nearly so prominent in the Old Testament as it is in the Epistle to the Romans. Moreover, as if to say that the Jews are right and that St. Paul was wrong, every man nowadays assumes that the story of the Garden of Eden is a myth, and, besides, is emphatic that the doctrine of original sin is a libel on human nature. Well, suppose that the Garden of Eden story is a myth, on the proper definition of myth? What is a myth? It isn't just a fanciful, untrue story, a fairy tale; though fairy tales can be myths, and be told with desperate seriousness. A myth is a story told about something which presumably happened before the dawn of recorded history, since history preserves no record of it, in order to try and explain how conditions as we know them today came about. The story, of course, was 'invented', but, in the circumstances, some sort of story seemed necessary. Take the story of the Fall: something is seriously wrong with man; how did it come about? The answer, any answer, to that question can only be given in the form of a myth. If you reject the myth, the Eden myth or any other similar myth; and if you reject the doctrine of original sin;

and if your view of the person of Christ is that He was just a very good man, the best man, of course, who ever lived; then your fundamental assumptions are more Jewish than Christian. I rather fancy that most people's are. But I am perilously near to preaching, and had better break off!

At any rate, we have cleared the air, and can now get back to the Old Testament. How, according to the Old Testament, did God enter into and maintain contact with the world? In the very early days stories were told of how He actually came down to the world, to see what men were doing, as in the Tower of Babel story (Genesis 11). Or it is said that He came to visit Abraham in his tent, and that Abraham entertained Him to a dish of veal! (Genesis 18). That, of course, was in the idyllic past, though the Jew who loves his Bible can still infer from such stories that there is no wide gulf between man and God, and that man—any man—has only to put his hand into the hand of God as a man's hand is clasped by the hand of his friend. Was not Abraham called 'the friend of God'? (Isaiah 41[8]). And did not God speak to Moses 'face to face, as a man speaketh unto his friend'? (Exodus 33[11]). Though, to be sure, not every man was a Moses. And even so, another story tells how once, when Moses asked to see the glory of God, he was told that no man could look upon God's face and live—'that were the seeing Him, no flesh should dare'; so God put him in the cleft of a rock as He passed by, and covered him with His hand so that all he saw was the aftermath of His glory, His back! (Exodus 33[18-23]). Other early stories tell how Yahweh appeared to men occasionally, as to the parents of Samson (Judges 13), and Gideon

(Judges 6), as 'the angel of Yahweh'. This 'angel' was not *an* angel, but '*the* angel' of Yahweh, Yahweh Himself in human form. Angels (in the plural) as we commonly picture them, were created beings, and they became more prominent, largely under Persian influence, in the later stages of Old Testament religion. The difference between Yahweh and His angel was a very transparent one, and when those to whom He appeared discerned who and what the angel of Yahweh was, they quite expected to die. Gradually, as such stories came to be regarded as too patently anthropomorphic, it became customary to think of God's revealing Himself to men in dreams (so to Jacob at Bethel, Genesis 28^{10-15}), or by some such sign as Gideon's fleece, which one night was to be wet with dew while the ground whereon it lay was dry, and on the next day dry while the adjacent ground was wet (Judges 6^{36-40}).

When we leave the mystic twilight of saga and emerge into the broader daylight of history, God's usual method of revealing Himself to man is by the prophetic 'word'. The word of Yahweh, as the prophets conceived it, was not something they had composed themselves; it was something that had been given to them by Yahweh. 'Yahweh spoke unto such-and-such a prophet, saying, Go, speak unto my people Israel, saying', or the like, is the usual formula. The 'word' of Yahweh has therefore an objective existence altogether apart from the personality of the prophet who utters it. Once it has been uttered, it is like an arrow sped from the bow; it must find its mark: 'For as the rain cometh down and the snow from heaven, and returneth not thither, but watereth the earth, and maketh it bring forth and bud, and giveth seed to the sower and bread to the eater; so shall my word be that goeth forth out of my mouth: it shall not return unto me void, but it shall accomplish that which I please, and it shall prosper in the thing whereto I sent it' (Isaiah 55[10-11]). But it can also be destructive: 'Is not my word like as fire? said Yahweh; and like a hammer that breaketh the rock in pieces?' (Jeremiah 23[29]). A distinction must be made between 'words' and the prophetic 'word'.

In the post-exilic period prophecy declined, and by about 400 B.C. it had practically ceased. In the time of the Maccabees the Jews were acutely conscious of this; the immediacy and intimacy of the prophetic word was a thing of the past, just as the direct manifestation of Yahweh Himself or of His 'angel' was a thing of the past. But although post-exilic Judaism was priestly in its emphasis rather than prophetic, we may not assume that it had any anti-prophetic bias. On the contrary, it is to the scribes that we owe the reverent editing of the prophetical writings, and the decline of prophecy occasioned a real sense of loss. Prophecy had done its work, but it had left as one of its legacies the conception of the prophetic 'word'. In time the 'word' became more or less hypostatized, that is to say, it came to be thought of as having a certain independent existence even as over against Yahweh Himself. Not, of course, that it was entirely separate from Yahweh. After all, it was Yahweh's word. The problem of identity and separateness as between Yahweh and His word is similar to that of the problem of the relation of the Persons in the Christian doctrine of the Trinity. But I think you can see that the conception of the 'word' of Yahweh was in some sort an anticipation of the Trinity, so far at least as the First and Second Persons in the Trinity are concerned. 'In the beginning was the Word, and the Word was with God, and the Word was God. The same was in the beginning with God. All things were made through him; and without him was not anything made that hath been made.' (These words call to mind the repeated 'And God said, Let there be . . .' in the story of the creation.) 'And the Word became flesh.' The prologue to the Fourth Gospel has sometimes been regarded as essentially Greek in origin and conception, going back to Plato, or at least to Philo, the hellenized Jew of Alexandria. That may be, to some extent; but it would never have found a place in such an intensely Jewish writing as the Fourth Gospel had it not been at least equally a development from Jewish forms of thinking. The conception of the 'word' of Yahweh was one bridge leading from the Old Testament to the New.

Another vehicle of contact between God and the world, and another bridge between the Old Testament and the New, is to be found in the conception of 'the spirit of Yahweh'. This is a very ancient conception, and goes back at least to the period of the Judges. In the books of Judges and Samuel we read of certain of the old Israelite hero-deliverers like Gideon, Jephthah, Samson, and Saul that the spirit of Yahweh 'rushed' (in the English Bible 'came mightily') upon them. In Judges 6[34] the expression is an especially striking one: 'the spirit of Yahweh clothed itself with Gideon' (so the Revised Version margin). The effect of this sudden descent of the spirit upon a man was to make him perform some feat of supernatural physical strength or martial prowess, as when it is said of Samson that 'the spirit of Yahweh rushed upon him, and he rent the lion as he would have rent a kid, and he had nothing in his hand'. Samson was not exactly a pattern of godly living, and it is not suggested that the feats he performed when under the control of the spirit were such as we associate with the Holy Spirit in the New Testament. In early Israel spirit was not yet thought of as 'holy' spirit. Indeed, only three times in the Old Testament is the spirit called the holy spirit, and that only in post-exilic times (Psalm 51^{11} and Isaiah 63$^{10-11}$). It is clear from the early stories that the 'spirit' was not something that welled up from within the man himself; it was not part of his natural endowment, but something external to him that descended upon him forcibly, and used him as its instrument. The phenomena accompanying its manifestations were of the kind that we associate with early prophetism, with its corybantic ravings that moved those who beheld them to amazement sometimes not unmixed with disgust. Nevertheless, since you have asked me to speak to you about the Thought of the Old Testament, 'especially as leading up to the New', it is worth noting that even in the New Testament there is usually something explosive or ecstatic about the workings of the Spirit. It was so on the day of Pentecost, and it moved scoffers to say that the Apostles were filled with new wine. We commonly think of the Spirit as quiet in its workings, 'that gentle voice we hear, soft as the breath of even'; but the earliest stories about the spirit of Yahweh in the Old Testament, notwithstanding that the conception of the spirit had as yet hardly begun to be moralized, have this in common with the workings of the Spirit in the New Testament, that the spirit is characterized by invincible, dynamic energy, rather than by the dreamy quietness that is induced by so many modern hymns about the Holy Spirit.

It would seem that the great prophets from the eighth to the sixth centuries reacted strongly against the conception of the spirit of Yahweh. There are, no doubt, two reasons for this: the first, that their conflicts with the so-called 'false' prophets led them to be suspicious of ideas which were associated with behaviour of the kind that could be induced by artificial means, such as music and dancing; the second, that they believed themselves to stand in Yahweh's counsel, so that Yahweh spoke directly to them without intermediary. But whatever may be the reason, the great prophets, with the exception of Ezekiel, who was psychically abnormal, and to some extent Isaiah, have surprisingly little to say about the spirit. Jeremiah, indeed, never even mentions the spirit, notwithstanding that he was, as we should say, the most spiritual of all the prophets. It is almost as though, during the greatest age of Old Testament religion, the conception of the spirit of Yahweh disappeared underground.

It re-emerged after the exile, but with significant modifications. In the first place, the conception of Yahweh Himself, under the influence of the prophets, had become completely moralized. And with the moralization of the character of Yahweh, everything that was associated with Him, including His spirit, came to be invested with moral properties. It is true that the words 'holy spirit', as such, are only found three times in the Old Testament, but other language that is used about it shows clearly that it was regarded as holy, and by the beginning of the Christian era the expression 'Holy Spirit' was quite at home in the religious vocabulary of the Jews. A second difference between post-exilic and pre-prophetic ideas of the spirit was that the spirit of Yahweh had now come to be thought of almost as a normal endowment and even constituent of human nature. The workings of the spirit were less intense than they were thought to have been in the earlier period, but they were more widespread. The moral life of the good man, the sententious wisdom of the wise, and even the skill of the expert craftsman were ascribed to the indwelling of the spirit of God (Exodus $31^{2f.}$). What once had been the monopoly—and that only for special tasks—of a few outstanding individuals, was now believed to be the abiding possession of ordinary devoted men and women. Indeed, in the creation Psalm (104^{29-30}) even the lower animals are said to owe their life to the spirit of God: 'Thou takest away their breath [in the Hebrew, 'spirit'], they die. . . . Thou sendest forth thy spirit, they are created.'

What I have said about the tendency to hypostatize the 'word' applies equally to the conception of the spirit of Yahweh. By the beginning of the Christian era the stage is set, so to speak, for the development of the Christian doctrine of the Holy Spirit. The great difference between the New Testament and the Old in regard to the doctrine of the Spirit is that in the New Testament the Spirit has become specifically the Spirit of Jesus.

Finally, a word should be said about the doctrine of 'Wisdom' in the later books of the Old Testament. In a late section of the Books of Proverbs (8^{22-30}) it is said of Wisdom that she—the word is feminine in Hebrew—was set up from everlasting, at the very beginning of the world. She was before the creation, a master-workman who was by God, and in whom He delighted continually. Clearly we have a similar semi-hypostatization to that which we have found in the conceptions of the 'word' and the 'spirit' of Yahweh. 'Wisdom' is a kind of middle term between 'word' and 'spirit'; its presence at the creation may be interpreted as relating it to both the other two, in view of the repeated 'and God said' of the creation story, and the statement that 'the spirit of God was brooding [Genesis 1^2, R.V. margin] upon the face of the waters'. In itself it seems more natural to relate it to the 'word' than to the 'spirit', but the language that is used about it relates it quite as much to the spirit as to the word; the spirit is often called 'the spirit of Wisdom'. It was outside Palestinian circles, in Hellenistic Judaism, that the Wisdom conception was most at home. This may be seen in the so-called Wisdom of Solomon, an apocryphal book which has many affinities with Greek thought. There, Wisdom is conceived almost as if immanent in the universe, a kind of universal cosmic force or world-soul. As such it was a speculative conception which lay outside the main current of Old Testament thought, and neither in post-Christian Judaism nor in Christianity itself has it the importance of the other two conceptions, the 'word' and the 'spirit' of God.

III

SALVATION

In the first lecture we were concerned with God and the general character of His relations with Israel; in the second with the world and the ways in which God maintained relations with it. It was obvious that the problem of the relation between God and man, already difficult in itself, was complicated by the fact that man felt himself to be in a wrong moral relation to God. In this third lecture, to which I have given the general title 'Salvation', it remains first of all to consider how the Hebrews thought of moral evil, and the remedies they supposed that God had provided for dealing with it.

There are about a dozen words in Hebrew descriptive of sin in its various manifestations. They may be divided into four groups: the first group denotes a missing of the mark, deviation from the right way—usually 'sin' in the English Bible; the second denotes an action that puts the doer of it in the position of being guilty before the law—hence 'guilt'; the third denotes the rebellion of a subject against a ruler—usually 'transgression' in the English Bible, not on the whole the most adequate translation, since rebellion is a more violent and flagrant offence than trespass; the fourth group describes evil for what it is in itself, 'vice'. Putting the four classes together, the late Dr. Wheeler Robinson wrote: 'We may summarize in a sentence by saying that sin is some deviation from the right way [i.e. group 1], which puts a man in the wrong before a judge [group 2], implies rebellion against a rightful authority [group 3], and is inherently vicious [group 4].' If we ask ourselves which of the four groups gets nearest to the heart of the matter, I imagine we shall say group 4, since it defines sin for what it is in itself, as something inherently vicious. That, however, is not where the Old Testament lays the most emphasis. After all, vice is a private thing, and in the Old Testament sin is always sin in relation to God; it is sin against God: 'Against thee, thee only, have I sinned', cried the Psalmist, even though the actual sin he was confessing may very well have been committed against some neighbour. On the whole, the Old Testament puts the emphasis upon sin as rebellion, wilful disobedience to God-given commands. That, and the emphasis, too, upon actions that put a man in the position of being guilty before the law, may seem to us—who so often in church hear sin defined as 'the offence against love', and the like—rather superficial, as though sin were nothing more than *lèse-majesté*, or mainly an affair of a celestial law-court. Well, I am not saying that the Old Testament conception of sin is the profoundest ever; after all, it is only the Cross that reveals sin at its most heinous, and it is because the Jew dare not face the Cross steadily that he is so comparatively optimistic about man's natural capacity for fellowship with God.

Anyhow, sin in the Old Testament is primarily rebellion, disobedience. But the Ten Commandments! they seem so elementary, so external, so obvious. Are they, indeed? When Jesus, in the Sermon on the Mount, seems to quote them almost disparagingly, He was actually making explicit what is implicit in them, as when He said, 'Ye have heard that it was said, Thou shalt not commit adultery: but I say unto you, that every one that looketh on a woman to lust after her hath committed adultery with her already in his heart'. Even Job, who lived under the old dispensation, had travelled more than half-way to the Sermon on the Mount when he said, 'I made a covenant with mine eyes; How then should I look upon a maid?' (Job 31¹). The best Jews knew very well that there are commandments within the commandments.

This, too, should never be forgotten when we think of the Ten Commandments: they were not moral precepts enjoined upon all and sundry, so that if a Gentile, conceivably, kept them, he had a passport to divine favour, and thereby purchased his acceptance with God; they were enjoined upon Israel, a people who already stood in the covenant-relation with God, as the outward sign and seal of the covenant. (I should perhaps say that it is by no means certain what the outward pledge of the original Sinai-covenant was; but that does not alter the fact that long before the fifth century B.C., our century of observation, that pledge had come to be accepted as the Ten Commandments.) What happened to a man, then, if he broke one of the Ten Commandments? The common notion is that he brought a bullock or a lamb, or a couple of pigeons, according to his means, and sacrificed them, and so was forgiven and all was well. Nothing could be farther from the truth. There were several classes of sacrifices in ancient Israel. One of them was called the sin-offering, and the ritual prescribed for it is detailed in Leviticus 4–5. There it is repeatedly said that the sin-offering was for the purpose of atoning for sins committed unwittingly or inadvertently. If a man sinned deliberately, 'with an high hand', as the phrase went, no sacrifice could atone for his wrong-doing (see Numbers 15[30]; Hebrews 10[26]); he was to be 'cut off', excommunicated, as we should say. Was there, then, no way of putting the matter right if a man knowingly and deliberately sinned? To be sure there was. There is a great deal in the Old Testament about forgiveness. If a man confessed his sin, God forgave him, freely. 'I acknowledged my sin unto thee, and mine iniquity have I not hid: I said, I will confess my transgressions unto the Lord; and thou forgavest the iniquity of my sin' (Psalm 32[5]). There is not a word about sacrifice in that Psalm. I am free to admit that the recital of the psalm may sometimes have been accompanied by a sacrificial offering; but even if it was, the offering was in no sense the purchase price of forgiveness. Forgiveness cannot be bought, or it would not be forgiveness. Forgiveness must be free, if it is to be forgiveness at all. Any sacrifice accompanying the confession of sin was the token of the offerer's sincerity, not a *quid pro quo* for forgiveness. I have not the least doubt that a man would often bring an offering in the expectation that God would overlook his known sins; but if he did that he was really going beyond what even the official religion permitted him to assume, and everyone knows that the great prophets condemned vain sacrifices in such strong terms that it has been plausibly argued that they condemned all animal sacrifice as such. It was much the same with the sacrificial system as it was with the Ten Commandments. The Ten Commandments together with the whole moral law which was a kind of supplement to them, and the sacrificial system together with the ritual laws which were a kind of supplement to it, were not so many ordinances which, if a Jew observed them, entitled him to assume that God would now accept and bless him. No! the presupposition underlying all Old Testament religion is that God is gracious, that He has of His free grace entered into covenant with Israel, and therefore now requires that Israel shall obey His commandments. Obedience to commandments and the due offering of sacrifices were not the purchase-price of grace. The Jew conceived himself to stand already in God's grace. Commandments and sacrifices were not supposed to admit him to the covenant, whereas previously he had stood outside it; they were the means whereby the covenant-bond might be maintained unbroken. That confirms what we already concluded in the first lecture, namely, that Old Testament religion was, in its essential principles, as much a religion of grace as New Testament religion is. The Ten Commandments in the Old Testament correspond to the Sermon on the Mount in the New. A poor comparison, perhaps, but the underlying principle is the same. The present-day emphasis in New Testament studies is that Christianity as it is presented in the New Testament is not a superior code of morals; it is the good news of what God has done in Christ to save men from their sins. And because God has met man in history, in the Cross and Resurrection of Christ, therefore man must now love God and love his fellow man. Old Testament religion is the same in principle: God in His grace entered into covenant with Israel at the Exodus, an event in history; therefore . . .! The Law is by way of corollary.

In what I have been saying about sin, grace, and forgiveness, the emphasis must have seemed to lie upon the individual. I have let it appear so, partly deliberately, in order to simplify the issues; because for us in our religious lives sin is almost entirely an individual thing, and so is forgiveness. To the average Christian it seems a little unreal—notwithstanding the present degradation of Germany—to speak of corporate or national sin, or of a nation (say) being 'forgiven'. But in Old Testament religion the emphasis is, on the whole, on the community, the nation Israel, rather than upon the individual Israelite. That is one reason why, in these days when we are coming to think increasingly in terms of community and national salvation, the Old Testament is so extraordinarily relevant. It tells us more about God's dealings with nations than the New Testament does. I do not mean that there was no individual piety in Old Testament times; there was. But on the whole Old Testament thought is in terms of the salvation of Israel rather than of the individual Israelite. That is one reason why it has so little to say about a future life for the individual, and then only in its latest pages. Speaking generally, the individual Jew would never have thought of his own salvation first, and that of his people second; it was sufficient for him that he should have a share in the redemption of Israel.

This opens up the wide subject of the Kingdom of God, with its related theme the Messianic Hope. As we saw in the first lecture, the conception of Yahweh as King was a very ancient one, and it gained in importance in post-exilic times. So strongly did the Hebrews come to feel that Yahweh alone was their true King that one set of stories about the foundation of the monarchy represents their demand for a king as rebellion against Him. This view of it is no doubt strongly coloured by disillusionment at the failure of the monarchy itself. But it had a religious basis. When at length the monarchy came to an end, any divided loyalty the nation may have felt as between the claims of the heavenly King, Yahweh, and the earthly king, disappeared. The High Priest now acted as Yahweh's vicegerent in spiritual matters, and even in worldly affairs so far as the imperial power—of Persia, Greece, or Rome, as the case might be—allowed the Jews to exercise self-government. Indeed, even during the days of the monarchy, the theory had been that the earthly king acted as Yahweh's representative. It was perhaps natural that the Jews should look the more to Yahweh as their King when they ceased to have an independent ruler of their own. The astonishing thing —and it is one of the most extraordinary triumphs of faith in history—is that, when they lost their political independence, the Jews, instead of losing their identity and their religion altogether, triumphantly asserted that their God Yahweh was King of kings, Lord of lords, and God of gods. By all the logic of events, according to the politico-religious ideas of ancient times, Yahweh had suffered a complete disaster in the political extinction of His people. The Jews did not accept that view of the situation. Instead, they came to believe that what their prophets had told them would happen was true—namely, that Yahweh had brought their kingdom to an end because they had rebelled against Him.

The conception of the Kingdom of God is parallel

in some respects with that of the so-called 'Day of Yahweh'. It appears that during the prosperous first half of the eighth century the Hebrews lived in expectation of a day when Yahweh would smite their foes and raise them high. Amos and other pre-exilic prophets who succeeded him insisted that 'the Day', so far from being a day of victory for Israel, would be a day of unmitigated disaster (cf. Amos 5^{18-20}; Isaiah 2^{10-22}; Jeremiah 4–6; Zephaniah 1^{7-18}). But after the exile 'the Day' came to be pictured as one in which disaster would overtake the nations that had spoiled and oppressed Israel. It was to be a day of judgement for the Gentiles and of deliverance for Israel (cf. Ezekiel 38–9; Joel 2^{28}–3^{20}; Zechariah 12, 14). Such of the Gentiles as survived 'the Day' were to be more or less compulsorily converted to Judaism. 'And it shall come to pass, that every one that is left of all the nations which came against Jerusalem shall go up from year to year to worship the King, Yahweh of hosts, and to keep the feast of tabernacles. And it shall be, that whoso of all the families of the earth goeth not up unto Jerusalem to worship the King, Yahweh of hosts, upon them there shall be no rain' (Zechariah 14^{16-17}). It is not a pleasing picture. Even the Deutero-Isaiah, who more than any prophet had a universal outlook, could picture the Gentiles as doing menial service for the Jews (Isaiah 49^{22-3}). More often than not the Jews shut themselves off from dealings with their neighbours, and had as little to do with them as they could. Marriages with non-Jews were forbidden, or even forcibly dissolved (Ezra 9–10). Occasionally a writer of more catholic sympathies, like the author of the Book of Jonah, protested against this exclusiveness, or the writer of the charming idyll of Ruth could remind his readers that even the great King David had been descended, three generations back, from a Moabite woman. We could wish that the Old Testament contained more writings of the kind. Nothing alienates the would-be sympathetic reader of the Old Testament so much as this general intolerance, as he conceives it to be, and he wonders why the Book of Esther, with its vindictive hatred of the Gentiles, should ever have been admitted into the Bible at all.

But before we condemn the Jews outright as uncharitable, let us try to understand the situation in which they found themselves. They had always, even in their days of political independence, been between the hammer of Assyria and the anvil of Egypt. Even though their prophets had condemned them outright, and even though in the first shock of the exile they accepted the prophetic judgement without question, as they picked themselves up out of the ruins of their national life they could hardly fail to be conscious that they were, relatively at least, more righteous than the heathen nations which had been Yahweh's instruments to bring about their disasters. There is hardly a more agonized cry in all literature than Habakkuk's 'Thou that are of purer eyes than to behold evil, and that canst not look upon perverseness, wherefore lookest thou upon them that deal treacherously, and holdest thy peace when the wicked swalloweth up the man that is more righteous than he?' (Habakkuk 1^{13}). To be sure, even such a justifiable attitude is capable of engendering self-righteousness, and there is no doubt that it did. But it is the Pharisee, not the publican, who lays himself open to it. The highest temptations are the subtlest and most deadly, but they are the highest; gross natures never come within sight of them. Moreover, one of the cardinal principles of Old Testament ethics is the doctrine of moral retribution, the doctrine, namely, that goodness is rewarded and evil punished. True, it does not always work out that way, but on the average it does, and it certainly appears reasonable that it should. We shall be coming back to it later, so far as the fortunes of the individual good man were in question. Meanwhile, here was a nation that had a loftier conception of God and a higher code of morality than any in the ancient world, but which on the principle of retributive righteousness certainly seemed to be having a rather raw deal. Not that they complained exactly; but they did expect that the day would dawn when God's righteous kingdom would be established, and when they would receive the due reward of their faithfulness.

Moreover, the Jews of the time of Nehemiah and Ezra, when the policy of separation from the Gentiles began to be rigorously enforced, did feel, and there is no doubt that they were justified in feeling, that the revelation that had been entrusted to them was infinitely previous, and that it might very easily be lost if they were complaisant in their attitude to foreigners. And, indeed, if they had not made vigorous efforts to canalize it, it might easily have been lost in the arid wastes of heathen tolerance. For us the highest virtue is tolerance; but one reason for that is that we value our religion so little. Monotheism has always inclined to being intolerant. 'The Lord thy God is a jealous God.' You cannot wholly believe in one God, and lightly brook the thought of rivals to Him. If Judaism had consented to deal with the heathen on their own terms, we might never have heard of Christianity.

Finally, on this question of the attitude of the Jews to the Gentiles—and I have dwelt upon it at what may seem disproportionate length for such a short course because, as I say, the modern reader of the Old Testament is so put off by it—religion is a concern of the community, the Church, quite as much as it is of the individual; and the only religious community that men were capable of understanding in ancient times was one composed of race or nation-state. (Nationalism is by no means dead yet.) Not until Christianity came into the world was it possible to conceive of a community, or Church, composed of Jew and Gentile, and in which there was neither Jew nor Gentile, but both were one in Christ. And, to do the Jews justice, when the danger that their faith might be engulfed in the surrounding heathenism was past, they began to be rather more charitable toward Gentiles than some passages in the Old Testament might lead us to expect that they would be. They came to admit Gentile proselytes, or converts, and even sometimes set out to win converts, always provided that the converts submitted to the requirement that they should observe the Mosaic law.

The problem of the moral order of the world, as based on the assumption of retributive righteousness, is sometimes perplexing enough, even when a whole nation is in question; but it is not insoluble. A nation lives on through its generations, and hope is usually eternal enough to expect that things will be righted some day. This was, and has ever since been, the persistent Jewish conviction that has kept alive faith in the Kingdom of God. But, for the individual the problem is urgent. He has only one life to live. If he is a wicked man and prospers, or if he is a good man and suffers, the contrast between desert and recompense is shockingly apparent. A community will always contain enough ne'er-do-wells to seem to justify the delay of its prosperity. There is not time in this lecture for even a summary history of Old Testament discussions on the problem of the suffering of the individual righteous man. I only touch on it here in so far as it involves the question of the place of the righteous individual in the expected Kingdom of God, and because it has an important bearing upon the emergence of the doctrine of a future life.

Concerning the hope of a future life the Old Testament as a whole has not much that is cheerful to say. Men like Moses, Jeremiah, and Job served God without expectation of eternal life. Occasionally a psalmist would cry out in something like bitterness: 'In death there is no remembrance of thee: In Sheol who shall give thee thanks?' Where and what was this Sheol? It was pictured as a cavernous place somewhere beneath the earth, to which men went when they died. They did not exactly cease to exist, but their life there—if, indeed, it could be called life—was but a pale shadow of the life they had lived on earth. It was supposed that social distinctions were still maintained in Sheol, but not moral distinctions. Alike for good and bad it was a dreary, hopeless place, a land of forgetfulness. Until quite late in Old Testament times it was thought to be outside Yahweh's jurisdiction. (The chief passages descriptive of it are Job 3^{17-19}; Psalm 88^{10-12}; Isaiah 14^{9-11}.)

Life presents no moral problems so long as the conception of God has not been moralized. Not until God is thought of as good does it occur to men to call in question the justice of things; they take life as they find it, without making bitter complaints. Further, not until the worth of individual personality is recognized do moral problems present themselves to the individual in any acute form. For this reason it was not until after the exile that the problem of the unmerited sufferings of individuals began seriously to engage the attention of Jewish thinkers. No one had thought it wrong that the family of Achan should be stoned together with their guilty father (Joshua 7$^{24-5}$). Even when the individual came into prominence it was at first assumed that the law of moral retribution applied to him as exactly as it did to the whole community. But experience, as the Book of Job insisted, showed plainly that sometimes it did not. And so long as Sheol awaited good and bad alike, the whole discussion inevitably arrived, sooner or later, at an impasse. It would seem that the first explicit statements that this present is not the only life arose out of attempts to relate the fortunes of individual Jews to the blessedness of the expected Kingdom of God. In two Old Testament passages, one of which is certainly, and the other probably, as late as the second century B.C., it is said that individuals will live again to share in the blessings of the Kingdom. One is Isaiah 26^{19}, which, in comparison with verse 14 of the same chapter, asserts that individual Jews will live again, whereas the godless heathen will not. The other is Daniel 12^2, where the implication is that righteous Jews will participate in the Kingdom, that the conspicuously ungodly will rise also, but to shame and everlasting contempt, while those who have been neither good nor bad are presumably to remain in Sheol. The details, you observe, are different; but both passages agree in speaking of a resurrection from the dead. That is the direction which, on Old Testament premises, anticipations of the life to come inevitably took. We have seen that the Old Testament did not think of man as an incarnated, immortal soul, but as an animated body; that the body, for it, was an essential constituent in human personality. Hence, when the Jews did at last come to believe in life after death they spoke in terms of the resurrection of the body, not, in Greek fashion, of the immortality of the soul. That is, historically, the reason why, when we recite the Creed, we say, not 'I believe in the immortality of the soul', but 'I believe in the resurrection of the body'. I am naturally tempted, of course, to argue the case as between the Greek and the Jewish-Christian conceptions; and I have no doubt that you would like me to. But that is a theme which lies outside the province of these brief lectures. I will content myself with one relevant observation, and that is that according to the thought of the Old Testament any life to come is of God's grace, not an inalienable portion of human nature.

Another, and in some ways higher, approach to the doctrine of a future life was the fruit of the piety of individual psalmists. It is not directly related to anticipations of the Kingdom of God, but it is convenient to mention it here. It is found at its clearest at the end of Psalm 73. Briefly, saintly souls found their communion with God to be such a real and precious thing that they could not conceive that even death would terminate it. They give no circumstantial details, and they do not, like the apocalyptic passages in Isaiah and Daniel, speak in terms of resurrection, nor, indeed, very clearly at all. Consequently, many scholars have doubted whether they really do speak definitely of a life to come. But the main direction, the logic, if I may use the word in such a connexion, of what they say is clear enough. We may put it that they appeal to a future life, not against the sorrows of this life, but on the ground of its highest blessedness, namely the blessedness of communion with God. That, surely, is where the main emphasis should lie, and also where the New Testament lays it: 'I am persuaded, that neither death, nor life . . . shall be able to separate us from the love of God, which is in Christ Jesus our Lord' (Romans 8[38f.]). The Christian is 'in Christ', as St. Paul puts it, and because Christ lives, he shall live also.

What was to be the place of the Messiah in the expected Kingdom of God? Messiah means 'anointed one', and the word was used in the days of the monarchy of the actual reigning kings, who were consecrated to their office by the ceremony of anointing. Curiously, it is not used, in the Old Testament itself, of the King who should reign in the future Kingdom. Indeed, in some descriptions of the Kingdom there is no mention at all of a king. Yahweh was to be King, either ruling directly, or, perhaps, through the High Priest. For example, the Book of Daniel has much to say about the Kingdom, but nothing about a Messianic King. (The 'Messiah' of the Authorized Version—'anointed one' in the Revised Version—in Daniel 9[25f.], refers to a High Priest who was in office not long before the Maccabean revolt; high priests were, in post-exilic times, anointed, as the kings had been in pre-exilic.) This lack of mention of a Messianic King in some descriptions of the Kingdom of God is one reason why the figure of the Messiah is not nearly so prominent in modern study of the Old Testament as it used to be. Another reason for the relegation of the Messianic hope somewhat into the background in modern study of the Old Testament is that it used to be assumed that the main function of prophecy, and indeed of the Old Testament as a whole, was to predict the coming of the Messiah, Christ. ('Christ' is from the Greek *christos*, 'anointed', and had therefore the same meaning as the Hebrew *messiah*.) It is now generally agreed that that was an exaggerated view. It had the more semblance of justification because the figure of the Suffering Servant in Isaiah 53 and the related passages was interpreted messianically, as a prediction of the death and resurrection of Christ. That view also has been largely abandoned by modern scholars, at least so far as it is to be understood as meaning that the prophet in Isaiah actually saw into the future, and had Christ specifically in mind when he wrote. But of that, again, in a moment. Meanwhile, if we distinguish between the Servant of Yahweh in Isaiah 53, and the political Messiah, the anointed King of the coming age, it would seem that the Messianic hope did not figure so prominently in the Old Testament as was once supposed.

Not that the Jews did not expect a coming Messiah; they did. The chief passages descriptive of him are those in Isaiah 9 and 11, to which may be added Micah 5^{2-5} and Zechariah 9^9. By the beginning of the Christian era some of the Psalms (e.g. 2, 72, 89, 110), which probably contain idealized descriptions of kings who reigned while the monarchy was still in being, had come to be interpreted messianically of the future King. The Messiah of passages like Isaiah 9 and 11 was not thought of as a divine being—the Jews with their almost fanatical monotheism would have thought it blasphemy to think of even the Messiah as equal in dignity with God Himself. But there are features in the descriptions which indicate that he was thought of as semi-divine; for example, 'His name shall be called Wonderful Counsellor, Mighty God, Father of Eternity, Prince of Peace' (Isaiah 9^6, R.V. margin). And if we give, as the Jews came to give, a Messianic interpretation to Psalm 2, we read, 'Yahweh said unto me, Thou art my son; this day have I begotten thee' (verse 7). This must be taken as meaning that the Messiah would be designated or installed as Yahweh's 'Son', as, indeed, kings in ancient times, both among the Hebrews and in the surrounding nations, were thought to be the 'sons' of God. With this difference, as between the Hebrews and their neighbours: by peoples like the Egyptians and Babylonians the sonship of the king to the god was supposed to be physical; for the Hebrews it was thought of rather as an adoptive sonship. There can hardly be any doubt that the words from heaven which Jesus heard at His baptism, 'Thou art my beloved Son', are reminiscent of the words of Psalm 2. The doctrine of the divine sonship of Jesus, therefore, has its roots in the Old Testament.

It remains briefly to say something about the Suffering Servant of the Lord in the Deutero-Isaianic passages, 42^{1-4}, 49^{1-6}, 50^{4-9}, 52^{13}–53^{12}. The question,

'Who was the Servant of Yahweh?' in these passages has given rise to more discussion, and prompted a greater diversity of answers, than any other single question presented by the Old Testament. The Servant has been variously identified with the nation Israel, or with some part of it; with individuals such as Moses, Jeremiah, Zerubbabel, and King Jehoiachin; and even with the Prophet himself. All these may be termed 'historical' interpretations; that is, they see in the Servant a community, or some individual, who had already lived in the past, or was a contemporary of the writer. My own view is that there was something of Israel in the portrait, something, too, of outstanding individuals like Moses, Jeremiah, and even, perhaps, of Jehoiachin, and also, doubtless, a good deal of the Prophet himself. That is to say, the portrait was a composite one. But in his highest thought the Prophet looked forward to an individual still to come, who should be supremely the Servant of Yahweh. In that sense the Servant was a Messianic, though not a political-Messianic, figure. On one thing there is practically unanimous agreement—namely, that Christ alone completely fulfilled the description of the Servant, and that He regarded Himself as its fulfilment. In that sense the passages may properly be regarded as Messianic prophecy. I mentioned just now the words which Jesus heard at His baptism, 'Thou art my beloved Son', and said that they were a quotation from the messianically interpreted Psalm 2. The voice went on to say, 'in thee I am well pleased'. These words, it is almost certain, are based upon the text rendered 'in whom my soul delighteth' in the description of the Servant in Isaiah 42[1]. 'Thou art my beloved Son, in thee I am well pleased': that sentence epitomizes the Messianic consciousness of Jesus as it became fully clear to Him at His baptism, and it is derived partly from the Messianic expectation of the Jews, and partly from the description of the Suffering Servant. The two streams, the Messianic hope and the Servant vocation, flow together in the Messianic consciousness of Jesus, and provide the clue to His ministry.

One thing more about the Suffering Servant: the last passage descriptive of him, Isaiah 53, gives what is for the Old Testament a unique solution of the problem of unmerited suffering. The sufferings of the Servant are not due to his own sins; they are borne, as we say, vicariously: 'He was wounded for our transgressions, he was bruised for our iniquities: the chastisement of our peace was upon him; and with his stripes we are healed. All we like sheep have gone astray; we have turned every one to his own way; and the Lord hath laid on him the iniquity of us all.' And, at the end of the passage, 'he bare the sin of many'. It was surely this chapter that Jesus had in mind when He said, 'The Son of man came not to be ministered unto, but to minister, and to give his life a ransom for many' (Mark 10[45]).

www.ingramcontent.com/pod-product-compliance
Lightning Source LLC
LaVergne TN
LVHW021623080426
835510LV00019B/2742